Protect Your Light

Cultivating Ramadan Habits into Our Daily Lives

Ismail Cisse

Published by:

Unit No. E-10-5, Jalan SS 15/4G, Subang Square,
47500 Subang Jaya, Selangor, Malaysia
+603-5612-2407 (office) / +6017-399-7411 (mobile)
info@tertib.press
www.tertib.press
@tertibpress (Facebook & Instagram)

Author	:	Ismail Cisse
Editor	:	Arisha Mohd Affendy
Proofreader	:	Norashikin Azizan
		Nadiah Mohamed Aslam
Cover designer	:	Abdul Adzim Md Daim
Typesetter	:	Abdul Adzim Md Daim

**PROTECT YOUR LIGHT:
CULTIVATING RAMADAN HABITS
INTO OUR DAILY LIVES**

First Edition: March 2024

CONTENTS

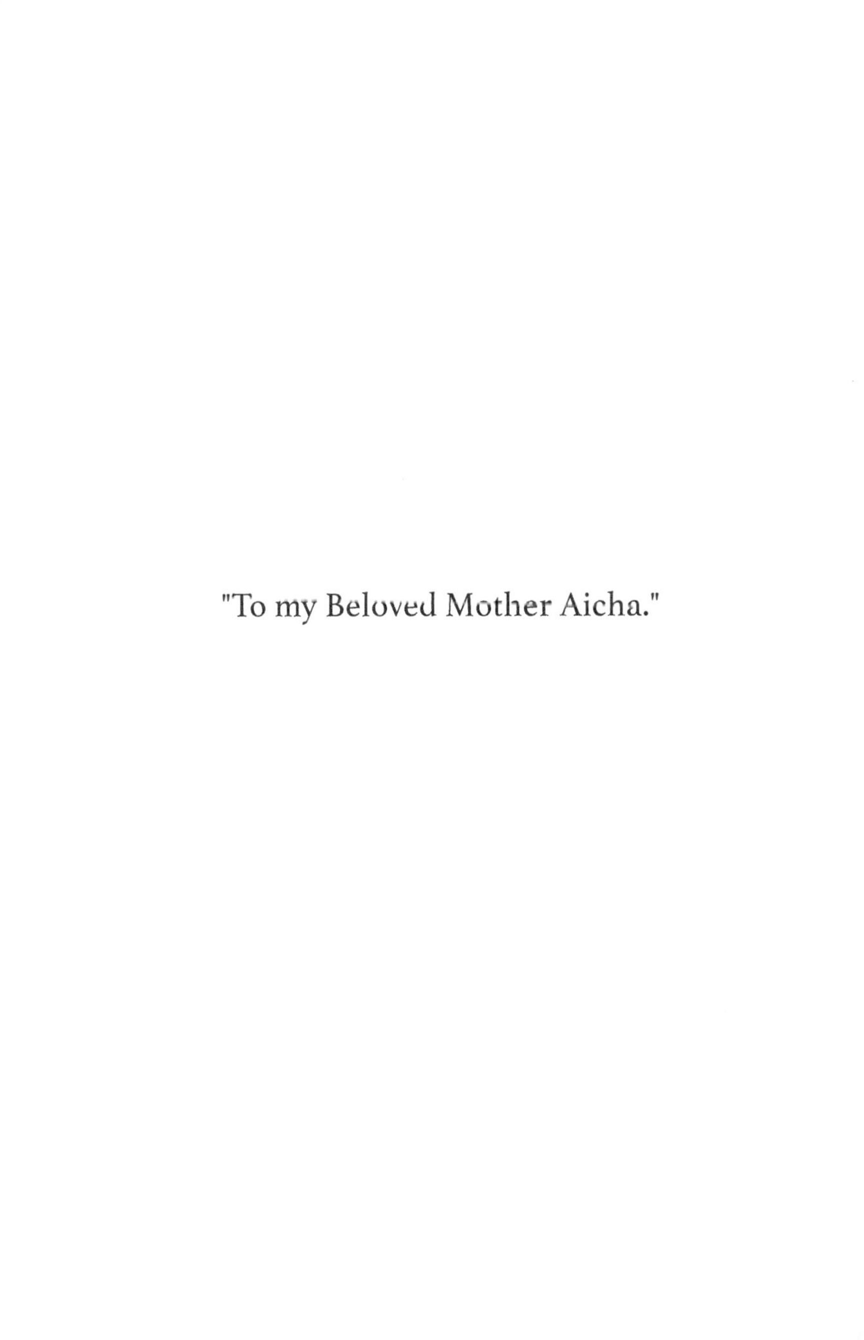

"To my Beloved Mother Aicha."

INTRODUCTION

All praises are due to Allah. May Allah's peace and blessings be upon the last messenger Muḥammad (s.a.w.). On Judgment Day, the sincere believers would shine with light radiating from their bodies, a light they cultivated during their worldly existence. Sins would be the cause of dim light for many on that day. Allah gave you a special opportunity to build massive light in Ramadan, get your sins forgiven, and get huge rewards.

During Ramadan, it's not just the mosques that are filled with light, but every Muslim household is shining with light. Ramadan serves as a training camp for Muslims, similar to how a boxer prepares in a training camp before a fight, to become mentally and physically strong. In the month of mercy, we discipline ourselves to resist our desires in obedience to Allah. The real challenge begins after the month of forgiveness, when the devils are unleashed.

This is the time to implement what you trained for, by combating your whims and desires. If you succeed during Ramadan, you can apply the same discipline every other month. I know it might not be easy but it's possible, that's why it's important to keep the flame of Ramadan alive in you.

We should strive to keep doing and maintain doing the good deeds that we used to—the positive habits that we cultivated during the holy month. The effort you invested in building your spiritual light throughout the fasting month should be preserved, and guarded against the encroachment of darkness caused by sins and desires. In this book, you will learn how to remain connected to the spirit of Ramadan, take complete control of your light, and not relapse into your bad habits after Ramadan. The month of fasting is designed to bring about positive transformation within us, fostering improvement and growth. This book has 3 parts like the month of Ramadan; mercy, forgiveness, and safety from the hellfire. I suggest reading one reminder each day, taking the time to contemplate its meaning, and implementing it in your life. Don't just stop there; revisit the book multiple times to reinforce these reminders. Your soul needs reminders the same way your body needs water. It's in our human nature to forget, and the only solution to that is to remind ourselves of Allah and the reason why we were created. *Shayṭan* does not take a break; he's always trying to lead us astray. Stay consistent in your efforts to do good as the Messenger (s.a.w.) said:

> "The type of work that Allah loves are the ones done regularly even if it's small."

(Sunan ibn Majah 4240)

I pray to Allah that you benefit from this book and that Allah makes my efforts purely for His divine sake. Written by the one who wishes what is best for you in this world and the next.

Tips On Getting The Most of This Book

1. Seek Allah's help and guidance for understanding and applying the learned concepts effortlessly.

2. Devote one day to each section, allowing time for reflection and practical application.

3. After reading a section, contemplate the content and ask yourself, "What is the best way and time to apply each suggestion?"

4. Use a pencil for the review section. Upon rereading, your perspectives may evolve with new insights.

5. Knowledge empowers, but its true potential is realised through consistent application in various situations.

6. Revisit this book multiple times after you have completed reading, to get a constant reminder.

Engage in reflections and self-inquiry. Use the quiz section as needed for guidance and explore quiz segments after the epilogue. These questions are crafted to enhance your self-reflection process.

Part I
MERCY

LOVE YOURSELF

Abu Bakr aṣ-Ṣiddiq (r.a.) said: "He who has a taste for the love of God can have no taste for the love of the world." [1]

Do you remember when you first fell in love with someone? You would do everything to satisfy that person, wouldn't you? You desire the best for your beloved and wish to shield them from harm. Despite any mistakes they may make, your love prompts forgiveness. Being in love can foster a greater sense of mercy and compassion towards your partner.

Allah's love for you surpasses your love for your partner. Just as you wish to protect your beloved from harm, Allah desires to shield you, and His commands are for your ultimate well-being. Every test you face is an opportunity that Allah is giving you to elevate your status. Allah is merciful towards you so be merciful towards yourself. Love yourself, and treat

1 Vehapi "The Book of Great Quotes", p 29

yourself like someone you love and care for.

How are you going to give love to others if you don't have love inside of you? You give from what you have, not what you don't have. If you have ill feelings, you will display negative emotions. Don't be so hard on yourself, speak empowering words to yourself. You have greatness within you, believe in yourself, and value yourself. Allah has put within you the ability to accomplish great things. All you have to do is to put in the work.

Love Yourself

Reflection:

UNLIMITED MERCY OF ALLAH

Allah said: "My mercy encompasses all things."[2]

Malcolm was born in 1925, in Omaha at a time when the only thing a black person could dream of was a shoe-shine man or a waiter. As a black man, you could not have big ambitions. Malcolm Little grew up in poverty, during his teen before he reached the age of twenty-one, he was living a criminal life. He could stay high for days, "opium, hashish, reefers, cocaine, all that stuff I used", said Malcolm Little.

In 1946, he was arrested by the police while picking up a stolen watch he had left at a shop for repairs. While incarcerated, he underwent a transformation, dedicating his time to learning and embracing the light of Islam. This metamorphosis led him to become a prominent advocate for human rights—el-Hajj Malik el-Shabazz, widely known as Malcolm X.

2 Qur'an 7: 156

Allah's mercy extends to even those who disbelieve in Him, deny His existence, insult Him and His Messenger (s.a.w.), or engage in sinful behaviour.

Despite their actions, Allah doesn't unleash immediate punishment such as striking them with lightning or having the earth swallow them.

He said in the Qur'an: "And if Allah were to impose blame on the people for their wrongdoing, He would not have left upon the earth any creature." [3]

Allah spreads his mercy towards all His creations. Don't give up on people, see them as who they could be and don't focus on their flaws. Advise the sinner and invite the one who does not believe.

---

3 Qur'an 16: 61

Unlimited Mercy of Allah

Reflection:

Be Merciful Towards Your Spouse

The Messenger (s.a.w.) said: "The best of you are those who are best to their women."[4]

A man came to ʿUmar bin al-Khaṭṭab (r.a.) to complain about his wife. When he reached ʿUmar's house, he heard ʿUmar's wife scolding him. He decided to return. On his way back, ʿUmar called him back and asked him, "I came to complain to you about my wife's behaviour but when I heard your wife's words I returned."

ʿUmar said: "I bear with her because of her rights over me. First, she is my protection from hell as she keeps my heart protected from the forbidden. Second, she is the keeper of my house, (especially) when I am away as well as the protector of my belongings. Third, she takes care of

4 Jamiʿ at-Tirmidhi 12:17

me and washes my clothes. Fourth, she nurses my children. Finally, she cooks my food and bakes my bread."[5]

You can't change your partner and make him/her perfect. Even our creator Allah, is not expecting perfection from us. Our spouse is a human being just like the rest of us—they have flaws. So treat them with kindness, love, and dignity, the same way you would like your children to be treated by their spouses later on.

5 Tanbih al-Ghafilin bi-Ahadith Sayyid al-Anbiya' wa al-Mursalin., p 517

Be Merciful Towards Your Spouse

Reflection:

Be Merciful Towards Children

The Messenger (s.a.w.) said: "O' Allah, be merciful to them (Usamah bin Zayd and Ḥasan ibn ʿAli at the time were children) as I am merciful to them." [6]

The Messenger (s.a.w.) would play with the little brother of Anas bin Malik (r.a.), Abu ʿUmayr who was a young boy, and (playfully) said to him: "what has the little sparrow done?" [7]

Teaching your children reliance on Allah and instilling good manners in them is one of the greatest gifts you can offer them. Show affection to your children through play

6 Ṣaḥiḥ Bukhari, 6003
7 Ṣaḥiḥ Bukhari, 6129

and kisses, conveying your love and care. While nurturing their self-esteem and imparting true values, don't let your love blind you to their misbehaviour—discipline and correct them when needed.

Teach children the meaning of 'no', and instil the importance of not having everything they desire. Emphasise respect for elders and proper behaviour in others' homes. Avoid spoiling them, maintain a healthy authority and treat male and females equally. Encourage positive conduct by rewarding them with praise or gifts.

Be Merciful Towards Children

Reflection:

Be Merciful Towards Animals

The Messenger (s.a.w.) said: "There is a reward for kindness to every living thing." [8]

The Messenger (s.a.w.) mentioned the story of a man who during his journey felt very thirsty, when he came across a well. He descended into it and drank from it to satisfy his thirst. Meanwhile, he saw a dog panting and licking mud because of excessive thirst.

The man said to himself, "This dog is suffering from thirst as I did." Therefore, he descended into the well, filled his shoe with water, and offered it to the dog to drink. Allah thanked him for that deed and forgave him. [9]

This man earned paradise by showing selflessness and considering the needs of a dog. Although Islam restricts

8 Ṣaḥiḥ Bukhari, 2466
9 Ṣaḥiḥ Bukhari, 2466

keeping dogs unless for specific reasons, that does not mean we should not treat them with gentleness or kindness.

A camel once complained to The Messenger (s.a.w.) about how it was treated by its owner. The Messenger (s.a.w.) then called the owner of the camel, and said:

> "Do you not fear Allah regarding this animal that Allah has put in your possession? Verily, she has complained to me that you keep her hungry and tired." [10]

Show kindness to animals, for each act of compassion earns you a reward, while every act of cruelty also carries its consequence.

10 Sunan abi-Dawud, 2549

Be Merciful Towards Animals

Reflection:

Be Merciful and Respectful

The Messenger (s.a.w.) said: "Whoever does not have mercy towards our young is not from us, whoever does not respect our elders is not from us." [11]

I once heard from a trusted friend about a non-Muslim man who served a Muslim family for 30 years, enduring mistreatment. The astonishing part of the story was the man's declaration: "I would never embrace the religion of these people (Muslims)."

> "Be merciful to those on the earth and the One in the heavens will have mercy upon you," said the Messenger (s.a.w.)[12]

We share one religion, united as brothers and sisters. Extend mercy to those younger and respect to those older. Treat your employees with kindness and humility. Today they are working for you, but what if the roles change

11 Jami' at-Tirmidhi. 1924
12 Musnad Aḥmad, 7073

tomorrow? Nothing is impossible.

Treat them the way you would like to be treated. Your wealth, colour, and family does not mean you are better than anyone. Allah said:

> "...the most noble of you in the sight of Allah is the most righteous of you. Indeed, Allah is Knowing and Aware" [13]

13 Qur'an 49: 13

Be Merciful and Respectful

Reflection:

Be Grateful For Being A Muslim

ʿUmar bin al-Khaṭṭab (r.a.) said: "If patience and gratitude had been two she camels, it would have mattered little on which I rode." [14]

Have you expressed gratitude to Allah today for the guidance bestowed upon you and your family? Consider the case of Muslims whose parents follow a different faith. Consider how you would feel if you were in their position.

The greatest blessing Allah has given to you is Islam, the greatest win is paradise, and the Qur'an is the guide towards paradise. The greatest loss is hell, and whoever does not have the Qur'an as a guide, would be among the losers. Appreciate your guidance, as some born Muslims have passed away in other religions.

14 Vehapi "The Book of Great Quotes" , p 83

Thank Allah for guiding you towards the book of mercy. "Verily, we were a disgraceful people and Allah honoured us with Islam. If we seek honour from anything besides that with which Allah honoured us, Allah will disgrace us," [15] said the leader of the believer, 'Umar (r.a.). If you are grateful, Allah would be pleased with you and increase you in many areas of your life (faith, health, sustenance, wisdom, and more).

15 al-Mustadrak 'ala al-Ṣaḥiḥayn, 207

Be Grateful For Being A Muslim

Reflection:

Be Grateful For Your Sanity

Allah said: "If you are grateful, I will surely increase you [in favour]" [16]

In his book, *Enjoy Your Life*, Dr. Muhammad Abd al-Rahman Al-'Arifi (r.a.h.), mentioned that he once went to visit a mental hospital, and he saw a crazy man who had been having epilepsy every five to six hours for more than 10 years. The second person that he saw would hit his limbs to a wall whenever he saw someone.

The last person he saw was an old man. Whenever they made him wear a cloth, he would tear it apart and then try to swallow it. When Dr. Muhammad wanted to leave, the doctor told him about the story of a businessman who used to be a millionaire. When he became mentally ill, his children brought him to the mental hospital.

16 Qur'an 14: 7

Ismail Cisse

Nobody knows how they will end up—making it crucial for your well-being to scrutinise what you allow into your mind and body. The prevalence of social media can lead to losing one's soul to its filth, contributing to the rising issues of depression and mental health. Take responsibility for caring for your mental, physical, and spiritual well-being by connecting your soul to its Creator.

Be Grateful For Your Sanity

Reflection:

Learn The Meaning Of The Qur'an

ʿUmar bin al-Khaṭṭab (r.a.) said: "Understand the teaching of the Holy Qur'an for it's the source of knowledge." [17]

During his childhood, Zakir Abdul Karim Naik used to have an excessive stammering problem. He was well-known for that at school. Sometimes he had to jump to let the words come out of his mouth. He had a dream of becoming a doctor just like his father. In 1987, his entire life changed when he heard Shaykh Ahmad Deedat preaching live—he was in his second year of studying medicine at the University of Mumbai. He was inspired by Shaykh Deedat and he then decided to learn about different religions such as Islam, Hinduism, and Christianity to answer all the questions that he had about religions. Presently, he is among the most influential Muslim scholars in the world.

17 Vehapi "The Book of Great Quotes", p 77

The Qur'an is a source of mercy and guidance; how can you fully benefit from that mercy without understanding it? While reading the Qur'an is commendable, grasping its meaning is even more beneficial.

That's what Dr. Zakir understood from a medical background to become a great Islamic scholar. He did not let his stammering problem stop him, and he did not make any excuses. What excuse do you have for not learning the meaning of the Qur'an? It does not matter the type of job you are doing. You can make time to learn the meaning of the Qur'an, even if it's one verse per day. Yes! You have the time, but you're simply not using it correctly. Suppose you're incredibly busy, and someone promises you a million dollars if you visit them at 10 am tomorrow. Without hesitation, you would make time for it. Dr. Zakir was busier but prioritised learning, so stop making excuses and start learning the meaning of the Qur'an daily.

Learn The Meaning Of The Qur'an

Reflection:

Be Satisfied with What You Have

ʿAli ibn Abi Ṭalib (r.a.) said: "Being deprived of something is better than being indebted to someone." [18]

The family of the Messenger (s.a.w.) sometimes spent days without food being cooked in their house, yet they were still content with Allah's degree. The Messenger said:

> "If any one of you looked at a person who was made superior to him in property and (in good) appearance, then he should also look at the one who is inferior to him, and to whom he has been made superior." [19]

Relying on external factors or desires for happiness is a recipe for misery. Even if Allah grants your wishes, the cycle

18 Vehapi "The Book of Great Quotes", p 40
19 Ṣaḥiḥ Bukhari,6490

continues, and you'll always yearn for more. When you are not able to appreciate the small things in your life, you won't be able to appreciate the big ones.

> "Wealth is not in having many possessions. Rather, true wealth is the richness of the soul," said the Messenger (s.a.w.) [20]

Express gratitude for the small blessings in life; find contentment in what Allah has provided.

Your soul becomes enriched when you appreciate what you have instead of longing for what others possess. Cherish the present, focus on the positives, and savour the sweetness of gratitude to Allah.

20 Ṣaḥiḥ Bukhari, 6446

Be Satisfied With What You Have

Reflection:

Pain Is A Blessing

Abu Bakr aṣ-Ṣiddiq (r.a.) said: "There is always more to any misfortune."[21]

The Prophet Ayyub (a.s.) lost all his children, wealth, and friends. Nobody wanted to be around him, he was left alone on the edge of the city, and only his beloved wife remained by his side to take care of him. Ayyub was patient and Allah rewarded him for his patience and gave him more than what he used to have. [22]

You are not the initial or final soul to face tests and rejections. The greater Allah's love, the more profound the trials. Since Allah holds His prophets in higher regard, He subjects them to greater tests. Thus, if you undergo pain—whether physical or emotional—recognise it as a manifestation of Allah's love and mercy. Allah guides His cherished servants through suffering to devoid of sin on the Day of Judgment.

21 Vehapi "The Book of Great Quotes" p 62
22 Tafsir ibn Kathir

It's important to be patient during your test. Don't waste your reward of patience by complaining and saying words that displease Allah, instead be positive about your pain and be strong, know that Allah would never put you in an unfavourable position. His help is near, and a great reward awaits you if you are patient.

Pain Is A Blessing

Reflection:

You Are Not an Angel

The Messenger (s.a.w.) said: "All of the children of Adam are sinners, and the best sinners are those who repent." [23]

"If you were not to commit sins, Allah would have swept you out of existence and would have replaced you by another people who have committed sin, and then asked forgiveness from Allah and He would have granted them pardon." said Allah's Messenger (s.a.w.). [24]

At times, errors and sins may occur despite your efforts, acknowledging your human frailty. Unlike angels, who unfailingly obey Allah, you lack infallibility, a quality

23 Jamiʿ at-Tirmidhi, 2499
24 Ṣaḥiḥ Muslim, 2748

reserved for prophets and messengers safeguarded by Allah from major transgressions.

As a human, imperfection is inherent, as perfection is reserved solely for Allah. The real question is what we do after we have committed the sin. The best of the sinners are those who repent, after committing sins. They don't dwell on it, they repent and strive to stay away from their sins. They don't want Allah to be angry with them.

You Are Not An Angel

Reflection:

Change Your Life

'Umar bin al-Khaṭṭab (r.a.) said: "Sit with those who constantly repent, for they have the softest of heart."[25]

During his youth, Malik bin Dinar was an alcoholic and was drowning in his sins. When his daughter passed away, Malik had a dream that it was Judgment Day, and he was running away from a powerful dragon that was chasing him. He saw an old man (his good deeds) and asked him for help, the old man was too weak to save him from the dragon (his bad deeds).

He ran on top of a cliff and found children there; he saw his daughter and she recited the following verse:

> "Has the time not come for those who have believed that their hearts should become humbly submissive at the remembrance of Allah and what has come down of the truth? And let them not be like those

25 Vehapi "The Book of Great Quotes" p 114

> who were given the Scripture before, and a long period passed over them, so their hearts hardened, and many of them are defiantly disobedient".[26]

When he woke up from sleep, he decided to change his life. That dream made him think twice about the type of life he was living, and he became one of the most famous scholars of hadith.[27]

The journey is not defined by its beginning but by its conclusion. Imperfection is universal. Instead of dwelling on the past, focus on crafting a positive conclusion to your narrative, as the power to shape your ending lies in the present.

Allah is the Most Merciful—He forgives all sins. Embark on improving your character now and strive to be the best version of yourself. Delaying repentance is a tactic of *shayṭan*; seize the opportunity for redemption promptly.

---

26 Qur'an 57:16
27 Kitab Tawabin, p 124

Change Your Life

Reflection:

Part II
FORGIVENESS

Seek Allah's Forgiveness Now

Abu Bakr aṣ-Ṣiddiq (r.a.) said: " Indeed God forgives major sins, so do not despair. And indeed God punishes for minor sins, so do not be deceived."[28]

A serial killer, who killed 99 times, was looking for redemption. He went to see a monk and told him about his crimes. He killed the monk because the monk did not see any hope in him. He then went to see another scholar and asked him if there was any chance for his repentance to be accepted, "Who stands between you and repentance?" replied the scholar. "Go to such and such land; there (you will find) people devoted to prayer and worship of Allah, join them in worship, and do not come back to your land because it is an evil place." On his way, the man died, and Allah forgave him of his past sins. [29]

28 Vehapi "The Book of Great Quotes", p 28
29 Ṣaḥiḥ Bukhari 3470

The first monk did not see any good in this man, while the second monk saw him as who he could be, not what he was nor did.

Death doesn't care whether you are young or old, rich or poor. Death does not give you a notification of its arrival. When your time comes, there is nothing that you can do. The duration of our lives is uncertain, so do not postpone seeking forgiveness and turning to Allah.

You may intend to transform into a better Muslim in your later years or during *ʿumrah*, yet if you meet your end before that, what response will you have before Allah? One of the great thinkers said, "You could have today, instead you choose tomorrow." All you have is now, not tomorrow nor yesterday, so take this moment and make the most of it.

Seek Allah's Forgiveness Now

Reflection:

FORGIVE YOURSELF

ʿAli ibn Abi Ṭalib (ra) said: "Forgiveness is the crown of greatness."[30]

The Prophet Musa (a.s.) prior to receiving prophethood from Allah, was involved in an incident where he unintentionally caused a man's death. At that moment, he sought Allah's forgiveness for his error, and Allah pardoned him. Musa closed that chapter of his life, moving forward without dwelling on his mistake.[31]

How are you going to advance in your life if you are always in the same chapter? To advance you need to turn the page and start that new chapter of your life. Allah forgives all sins even the ones that you can't forgive yourself for, so do not be hard on yourself. Return to Allah, regardless of how severe your mistakes are. Avoid dwelling on past errors; instead, learn from them. Every day is a new day, a new opportunity to do better. Focus on creating the best future for yourself, your family, and your community.

30 Vehapi "The Book of Great Quotes", p 105
31 Tafsir ibn Kathir surah al-Qasas

Forgive Yourself

Reflection:

SEEK FORGIVENESS FROM THOSE YOU HURT

Allah said: "Take what is given freely, enjoin what is good, and turn away from the ignorant." [32]

When you emotionally or verbally harm someone, and causing them to cry and call upon Allah against you, Allah will respond to their prayer. When you're wrong, admit it, set aside your ego and pride, and seek forgiveness from the person you've wronged.

While you can't change the past, you can start rectifying your mistakes in the present by seeking forgiveness and apologising. Take responsibility and avoid repeating the same mistakes. It's okay to be wrong; the problem lies in always wanting to be right, even when you're not. See things as they are, not as you wish them to be.

32 Qur'an 7:199

Seek Forgiveness From Those You Hurt

Reflection:

FORGIVE OTHERS

ʿUmar bin al-Khaṭṭab (r.a.) said: "Forgive people so that God may forgive you."[33]

There is nothing more painful for a mother than losing her child. Ask a mother who has lost her child about the pain. Samereh Alinejad experienced this agony twice. Four years after losing her 11-year-old son in a motorbike accident, she lost another son, Abdullah, who was stabbed and killed in a street brawl. Under the *shariʿah* law of retribution, the killer was sentenced to death. On the day of execution, as the killer stood blindfolded with a rope around his neck, hands tied behind his back, she initially refused to forgive him. However, at the last minute, the killer pleaded, "Please forgive me." The crowd witnessing the scene also sought forgiveness, and she requested the noose be removed from his neck.

33 Vehapi "The Book of Great Quotes", p 104

When we experience hurt, the natural inclination is to seek vengeance, to repay or escalate the pain inflicted upon us. However, this path is not worthwhile. Seeking revenge makes us akin to those who hurt us. As the emperor of Rome wisely stated, "The best revenge is not to be like your enemy." Aim to rise above, not to be on the same level or below.

Given the nature of human interactions, experiencing hurt is inevitable. It's essential to avoid getting upset over trivial matters that don't hold significance.

True forgiveness involves letting go completely. Saying "I forgive but I don't forget" or reminding someone of their past mistakes is not genuine forgiveness. Allah is asking those who don't forgive in the following verse:

> "Let them pardon and forgive. Do you not love that Allah should forgive you? And Allah is Oft-Forgiving, Most Merciful." [34]

You want Allah to forgive you, but you don't want to forgive others. When you grant forgiveness, the damage remains irreversible, yet it significantly alters the course of the future.

34 Qur'an 24: 22

Forgive Others

Reflection:

Don't Waste Your Reward

Allah said: "Kind speech and forgiveness are better than charity followed by injury..."[35]

"He who wants to publicise (his deeds), Allah will publicise (his humility), and he who makes a hypocritical display (of his deeds), Allah will make a display of him."[36] said the Prophet (s.a.w.)

When you engage in acts of kindness, refrain from boasting about them, as Allah recognises your intentions. Seeking people's attention diminishes the reward. Moreover, when assisting others, avoid using offensive language or demeaning them.

35 Qur'an 2: 263
36 Ṣaḥiḥ Muslim, 2987

> "When you offer any charity to a beggar, do it with humility and respect, for what you are offering is an offer to God" said Abu Bakr aṣ-Ṣiddiq (r.a.). [37]

Express gratitude to Allah for enabling you to assist others, as circumstances may shift, and you might also require their help. Life is unpredictable, and nothing is enduring. Maintain humility and kindness towards those you support.

---

37 Vehapi "The Book of Great Quotes", p 121

Don't Waste Your Reward

Reflection:

DON'T HARM OTHERS

The Messenger (s.a.w.) said: "The Muslim is the person whose tongue and hands do not harm other Muslims." [38]

There was a wealthy individual afflicted by intense pain in his left hand, disrupting his sleep at night. Despite undergoing various medical tests and following doctors' advice on exercises and medication, his condition showed no improvement. Seeking relief, he approached a shaykh for *ruqyah*, a Qur'anic healing practice. Hoping that the recitation of Qur'anic verses would alleviate the pain.

During his second visit, the *shaykh* said: "Maybe your ailment is a punishment for a sin you committed, perhaps you wronged a weak person or took someone's right. If you did any of this, then hurry to repent and give up the rights of others that you may have usurped. Seek Allah's forgiveness for all your past sins." Unpleased with what he heard "I have

38 Ṣaḥiḥ Bukhari, 9

never wronged anyone! I have never transgressed anyone's rights!" said the rich man and left.

He began reflecting on the shaykh's words, recalling an incident from a few years ago when he unjustly seized the land of a widow and her children. Seeking redemption, he approached the woman, seeking her forgiveness, and only upon her pardon did the man find relief from his pain. [39]

A teacher of mine once shared the wisdom of his Madinah-based mentor: "Choose to be among those who are oppressed among the servants of Allah, rather than those who oppress." If you can't be the eraser that erases people's pain, don't be the mosquito that sucks out people's blood.

39 Story in Book "Enjoy Your Life"

Don't Harm Others

Reflection:

You Can't Fight Fire With Fire

ʿUmar bin al-Khaṭṭab (r.a.) said: "When your spouse is angry, you should be calm, when one is fire, the other one should be water." [40]

If someone speaks or acts harmfully towards you, and that person is angered, refrain from escalating the situation. Maintain composure; responding with aggression will not lead to improvement but rather exacerbate the issue. Ultimately, neither party benefits, except *shayṭan*, as his goal is to sow discord and division among people. Allah said:

> "…Repel (evil) by that (deed) which is better and thereupon, the one whom between you and him is enmity (will become) as though was a devoted friend." [41]

40 Vehapi "The Book of Great Quotes", p 98
41 Qur'an 41: 34

Responding to wrongdoing with what is better doesn't imply silence and internalising resentment. It involves expressing yourself, conveying the truth with respect, choosing words carefully, and maintaining a composed tone.

While not easy, it is possible, requiring mental strength and resulting in emotional relief.

You Can't Fight Fire With Fire

Reflection:

Advise People or Correct Them

The Messenger (s.a.w.) said: "Religion is sincere goodwill..."[42]

There was a young man known for his sinful ways in the local community, lacking religious commitment. One day, while engaging in inappropriate behaviour with some girls, a shaykh observed him and discerned his intentions. The shaykh approached the young man, offering advice and cautioning against adultery. Touched by the shaykh's words, the young man repented and underwent a significant religious transformation. However, after two weeks, when the shaykh visited the young man, he learned that the young man had passed away that morning after the *fajr* prayer.

Persist in helping others, regardless of their flaws. While you may not have the power to alter someone's nature, you can offer guidance and supplicate for them.

42 Ṣaḥiḥ Muslim, 55

If the shaykh had not offered counsel, the young man might have perished in a life of transgressions, but the shaykh's advice brought about a transformative shift. Do not underestimate advising people. Aren't we the people that Allah said about in the Qur'an?

> "You are the best nation produced (as an example) for mankind. You enjoin what is right and forbid what is wrong and believe in Allah..." [43]

When providing advice, avoid assuming someone has disbelieved due to their actions. Maintain a positive outlook, considering that they may have made a mistake unknowingly. Refrain from self-praise during advice, and humbly acknowledge that you, too, are susceptible to similar errors. Beseech Allah to shield you from such mistakes and to assist the individual in forsaking their sins.

43 Qur'an 3: 110

Advise People Or Correct Them

Reflection:

IT'S NOT HEALTHY

"When anger arises think of the consequences" Chinese proverb

In 1986, Steven McDonald, a young police officer was shot by a teenager in New York's Central Park and that incident left him paralysed. After some time, he went on to say that. "I forgave (the shooter) because I believe the only thing worse than receiving a bullet in my spine would have been to nurture revenge in my heart."

Inquired about the health implications of unforgiveness, Professor of Psychiatry and Behavioural Sciences Karen Lee, shared with journalist Lauren Sandler that dwelling in a state of anger is akin to being in a perpetual state of adrenaline. The repercussions of not forgiving include elevated blood pressure, heightened anxiety, increased susceptibility to depression, and a compromised immune response. Such a prolonged state of negativity diverts one's energy in a detrimental manner. These changes elevate the risk of health issues such as diabetes and heart attacks.

Holding onto the harm others have caused puts you at risk, as you always carry the weight of their actions with you. It happened, accept it and move on with your life, it is part of your story, but not your entire story. Focus on the bright future ahead of you.

It's Not Healthy

Reflection:

It Gives Relief

"Let us forgive each other, only then will we live in peace" Leo Tolstoy. [44]

"Forgiveness felt like I was given a big pair of scissors to cut the tie and regain my personal power. It started with a choice, and then became a process," said the woman who lost her son in one of the biggest elementary school shootings in U.S. history. 26 people were shot dead. Yes, at first, she was angry at what happened to her son, but she decided to unshackle herself from anger and vengeance, so she forgave the killer.

Granting forgiveness to others for their mistakes alleviates a heavy burden from your shoulders and provides peace of mind. Forgiving those who have hurt you not only earns you Allah's forgiveness but also fosters forgiveness from those you may have hurt.

44 Quote found in "War and Peace"

It Gives Relief

Reflection:

Accept Societal Nature

Abu Bakr aṣ-Ṣiddiq (r.a.) said: "cooperate with one another and do not bare grudges of jealousy." [45]

While coexisting with others, experiencing hurt is inevitable. In the same way it's impossible for a fish to be inside water and not be touched by it. It is unrealistic to escape people's negative actions and words, no matter your efforts or words. Even if you were to live alone in the mountains, you might be spared from physical harm, but opinions and comments would still circulate about your solitary lifestyle, demonstrating that avoiding criticism entirely is impossible.

There's no need to escape; rather, accept the reality of society. The crucial aspect is understanding the purpose behind your actions. You are not in this world to seek the pleasure of the people, but to seek the pleasure of the

45 Vehapi "The Book of Great Quotes" p 109

Creator of all creations. What Allah thinks of you is more important than what people think of you. The Messenger (s.a.w.) said:

> "The believer who mingles with the people and endures patience over their harm, is better than one who does not mingle with the people nor endures patience over their harm."[46]

Constantly bear in mind our human nature, prone to hurting or upsetting each other. Reflect on your actions daily, asking, "Whom have I unintentionally hurt?" Embrace imperfection, practice forgiveness, maintain connections despite mistakes, treasure positive moments, and overlook the negatives in others.

46 Jami' at-Tirmidhi 2507

Accept Societal Nature

Reflection:

Don't Be Offended By The Truth

Abu Bakr aṣ-Ṣiddiq (r.a.) said: "The greatest truth is honesty and the greatest falsehood is dishonesty."[47]

A genuine friend will always speak the truth for your well-being, as they genuinely care about you. Conversely, a deceitful friend won't bother with the truth, prioritising personal gain and likely letting you down when their interests no longer align with yours. If someone highlights a flaw in your actions or suggests ways for improvement, appreciate their concern and consider it as a valuable opportunity for self-betterment.

The philosopher Marcus Aurelius said: "It's better if anyone can prove and show to me that I think and act in error, I will gladly change it for I seek the truth, by which no

47 Vehapi,"The Book of Great Quotes", p 43

one has ever been harmed, the one who is harmed is the one who abides in deceit and ignorance." Don't be offended by the truth, seek the truth; don't seek what you want to hear.

Don't Be Offended By The Truth

Reflection:

Don't Be Bitter

The Messenger (s.a.w.) said: "The strong is not the one who overcomes the people by his strength, but the strong is the one who controls himself while in anger." [48]

The tiniest seed of resentment can grow into a poisonous tree. Initially inconspicuous, these small resentments accumulate and turn into something much more significant. A person harbouring bitterness may appear composed externally, but internally, they're on the verge of erupting with pent-up emotions. Their hearts brim with anger, and some may find it difficult to love. The detrimental aspect of harbouring bitterness is that it offers no benefits; it only inflicts harm and self-destruction. It's crucial to eliminate the roots of bitterness before they take hold.

48 Ṣaḥiḥ Bukhari 6114

The Canadian clinical psychologist, Jordan Peterson, identified two primary reasons people overcome bitterness. The first involves personal growth, urging individuals to mature, cease complaining, and assume responsibility for their lives. The second reason is addressing oppression; if someone acts as a tyrant towards you, it's essential to speak up. When someone does something harmful, communicate with them to prevent future occurrences. Whether the action was unintentional or deliberate, initiating a conversation can prevent a cycle of hurt, bitterness, anger, and the desire for revenge.

Don't Be Bitter

Reflection:

DON'T HATE

"Whoever opts for revenge should dig two graves." Chinese proverb

A gathering of elderly individuals over the age of sixty embarked on a hunting expedition. Along the way, a disagreement ensued over a parcel of land claimed by one as his grandfather's. The landowner, angered by the assertion, aimed his gun at his friend's head, threatening, "By Allah, if I catch you near my land, I'll discharge this (indicating his gun) into your head." Fortunately, the other companions intervened to prevent a physical altercation.

Consumed by animosity, the individual who faced the threat with the gun couldn't find peace that night. Driven by a desire for vengeance, he armed himself with an AK47 the next morning, intending to kill the other person. He lurked near the man's workplace, positioned behind a tree, and aimed the gun at the elderly individual, firing three shots that pierced through the old man's skull.

Subsequently, the assailant turned himself to the police, confessing, "I murdered so-and-so, thereby easing my conscience. You may now execute me, incinerate me, or incarcerate me. Do as you see fit!" However, during the investigation, the perpetrator was astounded; he lost consciousness upon discovering that he had mistakenly killed a different elderly man, not the one he had intended to target. [49]

"Hate is a disease which may destroy your enemy, but will also destroy you in the process," said Eddie Jaku, an old holocaust survivor. Deliberately causing harm to someone ultimately inflicts more damage on yourself. "Any person capable of angering you becomes your master. He can anger you only when you permit yourself to be disturbed by him," said the philosopher Epictetus. It's not worth it; release the hatred. True enslavement occurs when someone governs what you feel within. Don't be a captive to your emotions; learn to regulate them, or they will dominate you.

49 Story in Book "Enjoy Your Life"

Don't Hate

Reflection:

DON'T BLAME ALLAH

Allah said: "And We will surely test you with something of fear, and hunger, and a loss of wealth, and lives and fruits. But give good tidings to the patient." [50]

Before starting their journey Khidr (a.s.) told to prophet Musa (a.s.): "You will not be able to have patience with me (67) And how could you have patience with that which your knowledge does not encompass?" (68)

Musa replied "You will find me, if Allah so wills, patient. And I will not disobey you in any command" (69).

"Then, if you follow me, ask me not about anything till I myself mention it to you." (70) added Khidr (a.s.). [51]

50 Qur'an 2: 155
51 Qur'an 18: 67-70

During their journey, Musa (a.s.) first observed him damaging a boat and inquired, "Have you damaged it to drown its people?" Later, when he witnessed him killing a young boy, Musa (a.s.) remarked, "Have you killed a pure soul for other soul? You have surely brought an evil thing." said Musa (a.s.).

Finally, he and Musa (a.s.) repaired a wall that was on the verge of collapse. After completing the construction, Musa (a.s.) said, "If you wish, you may ask a reward for it." Khidr (a.s.) stopped their journey and he clarified to Musa (a.s.) the motives behind his actions.

He damaged the ship so that the owner could keep it; there was an oppressor king who was seizing every ship by force. He killed the boy because if he grew up, he was going to become an oppressor to his parents (that were religious), and a disbeliever. Allah replaced that boy with another son who was purer and closer to mercy.

He built the wall because under that wall were some treasures for two orphans whose father was a pious person, so Allah willed that they should reach adulthood and take out their treasure. [52]

Every occurrence has a purpose, guided by divine wisdom within each trial. It's possible that what you desire might be detrimental, and Allah, in His love for you, safeguards you from harm. He understands what is beneficial for you and

52 Tasfsir ibn Kathir surah Kahf Q18: 66-82

will not place you in an unfavourable situation. Place your trust in His divine wisdom with complete submission to His decree. Life is a series of tests, but always bear in mind that Allah does not burden a soul beyond its capacity.

Difficulties are designed to transform us, fostering growth. The absence of challenges equates to a lack of development. Experiencing tough times doesn't signify that Allah dislikes or wishes to punish you. Instead, view every trial as a chance to evolve and improve. When you stray from the worship of Allah, He may subject you to a test to guide you back to Him. Rather than blaming Allah for your circumstances, express gratitude for the chance He has given you to transform. Sometimes God doesn't alter the situation you're in. Instead, He transforms you to build strength, enabling you to navigate the storm.

Don't Blame Allah

Reflection:

Part III

SAFETY FROM HELLFIRE

Be Productive

The Messenger (s.a.w.) said: "Be eager for what benefits you..."[53]

Certain individuals exist in a state of unawareness, they are alive yet spiritually, mentally, physically, and financially lifeless. This condition stems from their profound lethargy, and a reluctance to invest effort in personal growth. Persistently perceiving themselves as victims, they habitually attribute their circumstances to external factors. Laziness, the primary culprit, invites concerns and despondency, whereas an engaged and active approach to life results in contentment and a sense of accomplishment.

Nobody is obligated to fulfil your needs. The responsibility for achieving your goals rests squarely on your shoulders. It is crucial to take charge of your own life. A historical example illustrating this principle comes from the time of Caliph 'Umar (r.a.) when he discovered young

53 Ṣaḥiḥ Muslim 2664

individuals loitering in the mosque without actively seeking sustenance. In response, he expelled them, from the mosque and said, "Go out and seek sustenance, for the sky does not rain gold and silver." [54]

You have the choice to be strong or weak. Choose to be strong and productive in everything that you do as the strong believer is more beloved to Allah than the weak believer. Be the best at what you do. Choose to be someone that other people can rely on when they need help.

54 Story in Book "Don't be Sad'

Be Productive

Reflection:

Don't Go Back To Haram

Abu Bakr aṣ-Ṣiddiq (r.a.) said: "Do not follow vain desires for verily he prospers who is preserved from lust, greed and anger." [55]

Imagine the emotions of a prisoner after serving a 30-year sentence, finally testing freedom. Similarly, some Muslims may feel confined to the acts of worshipping during Ramadan, and finding liberation afterward to indulge in whims and desires. During Ramadan, mosques are bustling, and the Qur'an echoes in the air. However, post-Ramadan, only a handful persist in righteous deeds and avoiding the forbidden. Be part of the minority; resist the pull of the majority. Without striving against your desires, steering clear of the forbidden becomes a challenge.

Recognise that as Muslims, our freedom is nuanced. While we have the freedom of choice, we are not entirely

55 Vehapi "The Book of Great Quotes" p 39

free; we owe our existence to Allah. He is our Creator, and as the slaves of Allah, we have responsibilities and limits to observe. Everyone is a slave to something. Being subservient to something implies serving and prioritising it above all else. Becoming a slave to money, desires, or anything other than Allah compromises true freedom.

Remember that we worship the Lord of Ramadan, not Ramadan. Certainly, Ramadan has come to an end, but it's crucial to continue remembering Allah, exert efforts to avoid the forbidden, and engage in more righteous deeds to enhance the light that will illuminate your path on Judgment Day. Be vigilant against the deception of *shayṭan*. Remember that you possess the strength within to combat your desires. With Allah by your side, seek His assistance to steer clear of the forbidden.

Don’t Go Back To Haram

Reflection:

Keep On Doing Good

Allah's Messenger (s.a.w.) said to me, "O' ʿAbdullah! Do not be like so and so who used to pray at night and then stopped the night prayer." [56]

Continue doing good even when others cease to treat you well. Keep giving, without expecting anything in return—understanding that your reward comes from Allah, who observes and knows all things. Consistency is key; Allah values deeds that are done regularly, even if they are small.

Persist in the positive habits you developed during Ramadan, such as praying the night prayer, reading more Qur'an, giving charity, and avoiding sinful actions. Even if you must slow down a bit, remain consistent. The following saying is attributed to Bruce Lee the legendary martial artist, "I fear not the man who has practised 10,000 kicks once, but I fear the man who has practiced one kick 10,000

56 Ṣaḥiḥ Bukhari, 1152

times,". Keep moving forward; this world is not a place for leisure but a realm to work towards building your hereafter. Rest awaits you in the eternal paradise, so never lose hope or give up.

Keep On Doing Good

Reflection:

TYPE OF DEATH

Angel Jibril (a.s.) said: "O' Muhammad, live as you wish, for you will surely die. Work as you wish, for you will surely be repaid. Love whomever you wish, for you will surely be separated..." [57]

Shaykh Abdul-Hamid Kishk was one of the most eminent Islamic speakers of the twentieth century, He gained recognition as an activist and author, renowned for his impactful sermons and his outspoken position against injustice and oppression in the Muslim world. He frequently supplicated to Allah, saying, "O' Allah, allow me to live as a scholar, die as a scholar, and resurrect me in the state of prostration." On the morning of Friday, December 6, 1996, his wish was fulfilled as he passed away in a state of prostration.

57 al-Muʿjam al-ʾAwsaṭ lil-Ṭabarani 4278

You shall die upon what you live on. The ancient Greeks expressed this idea with the phrase '*Memento Mori*' (remember thou art mortal). Keep death in your consciousness, for nothing in this world is everlasting. Frequently, we hear about the passing of others, but one day it will be our turn, and someone else will learn of our departure. What preparations have you made for that inevitable day, considering it can arrive at any moment?

People have met their end while engaged in various activities—singing, dancing, and committing greater sins like adultery. Conversely, some have departed while reciting the Qur'an, praying, and engaging in virtuous deeds. Reflect on the way you want to meet your end. Your life's trajectory determines your death.

In the grave, there are no relations, partners, children or wealth—only you and your deeds. Start living in a manner that aligns with the death you desire.

Type Of Death

Reflection:

Be Alive

The Prophet (s.a.w.) said: "The example of the one who remembers his Lord, and the one who does not remember Him is like the example of a living and a dead person."[58]

Allah said: "O' you who have believed, respond to Allah and to the Messenger when he calls you to that which gives you life. And know that Allah intervenes between a man and his heart and that to Him you will be gathered."[59]

Peace of mind is unattainable without a connection to the Creator of the mind. To experience peace, establish a

58 Riyad aṣ-Ṣaliḥin 1434
59 Qur'an 8: 24

connection with the Book of Allah and maintain a constant remembrance of Him. Allah said:

> "By the remembrance of Allah hearts are assured." [60]

Remembrance of Allah not only brings peace but also revitalises your spirit. As you remember Allah, He reciprocates by remembering you. Taking one step towards Him results in Him taking many steps towards you. It's crucial to recognise that Allah doesn't need you; rather, you are dependent on Him. The remembrance of Allah is the source of true vitality and turning away from it leads to a life of misery devoid of peace. The more you remember Allah, the more spiritually alive you become.

60 Qur'an 13: 28

Be Alive

Reflection:

GUIDANCE

ʿUmar bin al-Khaṭṭab said: "Don't forget your own self while preaching to others." [61]

A renowned monk devoted sixty years to worshipping Allah, attaining such spiritual closeness that his supplications could bring about cures through divine intervention. *Shayṭan*, unable to lead him astray directly, sought an alternative approach. The devil influenced a woman, making her mentally unstable. *Shayṭan* then convinced her brothers to take her to the monk for healing. She stayed in the monk's house for some time, and eventually, an unexpected event transpired.

The revered monk succumbed to the deception of *shayṭan*, engaging in adultery with the afflicted woman who later became pregnant. To conceal his transgression, he resorted to murdering her. When the woman's family discovered the heinous act, they sought justice from the king for their sister's plight.

61 Vehapi "The Book of Great Quotes" p 91

The king, upon learning of the monk's abhorrent actions, decreed the penalty of death. Prior to the execution, *shayṭan* approached him and said, "I have been trying to find ways to deceive you, and I finally found one, prostrate before me and I'll save you." The monk, succumbing to the deceit, prostrated before *shayṭan*. However, *shayṭan*, disavowing him, declared:

> "I am free of you; I fear Allah, the Lord of the Alamin (mankind, jinn, and all that exists)" [62]

In the end, the monk died as an idolater, having associated partners with Allah. [63] Don't take your faith for granted! Ask Allah to guide you to the straight path, and ensure that your actions align with the guidance you seek. Maintain humility, as it elevates your status with Allah. Seek Allah's guidance, for the heart is not stable; it's always changing, that's why our beloved Messenger's most recited prayer was: "O' Turner of the hearts, keep my heart firm upon Your religion." [64]

62 Qur'an 59: 16
63 Tafsir Ṭabari
64 Jamiʿ at-Tirmidhi, 2140

Guidance

Reflection:

Use Your Tongue Wisely

ʿAbdullah bin Masʿud (r.a.) said: "Nothing on earth is in greater need of a lengthy prison sentence than the tongue." [65]

The tongue may be small in size, yet its impact can be enormous for those who do not use it wisely. Consider how many individuals have faced trouble due to their words. We are equipped with two ears to listen more and only one tongue to speak less with. The Messenger (s.a.w.) said:

> "A person utters a word thoughtlessly (i.e., without thinking about its being good or not) and, as a result of this he would fall down into the fire of Hell deeper than the distance between the east and the west." [66]

65 Al-Muʿjam al-Kabir 8745
66 Riyad aṣ-Ṣaliḥin 1514

The tongue has been the cause of many people entering Hell, that's why it's important for you to think before you speak. The Messenger (s.a.w.) said:

> "He who believes in Allah and the last day must either speak good or remain silent "[67]

A kind and positive word is considered an act of charity. Instead of using your tongue to harm, utilise it to earn rewards by remembering Allah.

Choose your words to uplift, not to bring others down. If you don't have something valuable to say, it's better to remain silent.

---

67 Ṣaḥiḥ Bukhari 6019

Use Your Tongue Wisely

Reflection:

BACKBITING

ʿUthman bin ʿAffan (r.a.) said: "A backbiter harms three individuals firstly he harms himself, secondly the person he is addressing, and thirdly the person whom he is backbiting."[68]

Imagine the feeling of losing all your possessions—money, cars, houses being distributed among people, making you face bankruptcy. Now, picture on Judgment Day, your hard-earned good deeds being distributed among others. Your pilgrimage reward goes to your uncle, the charity you donated goes to your cousin, the reward for fasting goes to your mother-in-law, and the reward for feeding the poor goes to your daughter-in-law. All lost because you spoke ill of them.

Before you start speaking about someone behind their back, remember that you are giving away your good deeds. Wouldn't it be better if you called them and gave them advice to help them become better?

---

68 Vehapi "The Book of Great Quotes", p 50

Backbiting

Reflection:

Protect Yourself And Your Family

Allah said: "O' you who have believed, protect yourselves, and your families from a Fire."[69]

The fruits of turmoil have flourished in this century. The multitude are following the antichrist, they attempt to plant seeds of incorrect beliefs in the minds of our children from a young age through various media channels and social platforms. As a parent, it is your duty to shield yourself and your family. If you take no action and remain passive, the consequences of this turmoil will infiltrate your family. By the time you recognise it, it may be too late.

You may find your children, husband, or spouse adopting surprising thoughts and behaviours due to the influence of these tribulations. It's crucial to uproot the tree

69 Qur'an 66: 6

of turmoil while it's still small. Engage with your family, provide guidance, and revive the teachings of the Prophet (s.a.w.) together. Read the Qur'an and hadith collectively, even if it's just once a week. It can serve as a protective measure against the influence of *shayṭan*. If you don't, *shayṭan* would make sure to mess up with their beliefs about Islam.

Protect Yourself And Your Family

Reflection:

Jannah Is Under Her Feet

ʿAbdullah bin Mubarak (r.a.) said: "If you people wish to backbite, then backbite your own parents, so that your rewards does not go out to a stranger, rather to them."[70]

You can never repay your parents for what they did for you. During *ḥajj,* a man carried his mother on his back while doing the circumambulation of the Kaʿbah. "O' Ibn ʿUmar, do you think I have repaid her?" asked the man, "Not even for a single pang of pregnancy." Ibn ʿUmar (r.a.) replied. [71]

When the entire world is against you, she remains your best friend. Even if the entire world rejects you, she will always love you. Your mother is a rare flower that needs to be watered by love. You can't pay back everything that she did

70 The life of Abdullah Bin Mubarak, p 42
71 Al-Adab al-Mufrad, 11

for you. During your arrival into this world, you caused her pain and made her bleed, yet she loves you unconditionally. This is genuine love, and you don't need to search for it; you already possess it.

She is your gateway to paradise. Therefore, take care of her, cherish her, and express your love consistently. Shower her with gifts, speak words of affection, and treat her with respect. Don't bring sorrow into her life, and don't wait for a special occasion to demonstrate your care for her as your paradise lies under her feet.

Jannah Is Under Her Feet

Reflection:

CHOOSE THE ONE THAT WOULD TAKE YOU TO *JANNAH*

The Messenger (s.a.w.) said: "Marry the religious woman."[72]

A religious woman will encourage you to go to the mosque when it's time to pray, and she'll wake you up for night prayers, prioritising Allah over everything, even her love for you. Despite being human and imperfect, she strives to uphold her religious duties. Similarly, a religious man will honour the rights of his wife and show her mercy. A relationship with individuals who understand and practice Islam as it should be brings more peace, blessings, harmony, and love.

A healthy relationship should bring peace, as marriage without peace is of little value. It's crucial to reflect before

72 Ṣaḥiḥ Bukhari 5090

making a choice, avoiding being blinded by love. People can't be changed by others; the change must come from within. The high divorce rate in the Muslim community is often attributed to marrying for the wrong reasons. Initially, relationships may seem wonderful, but as time passes, flaws become apparent, and without the ability to handle them, problems arise. Don't marry someone, and then expect the person to change.

Choose The One That Would Take You To Jannah

Reflection:

FEAR ALLAH WHEN ALONE

The Messenger (s.a.w.) said: "Whatever Allah hates for you to do, then do not do it in private." [73]

On the Day of Judgment, a gathering of individuals who engaged in fasting, night prayers, and various virtuous acts will discover that their substantial rewards, akin to mountains, will disintegrate like dust. This is due to the fact that, in the solitude of darkness when no one was observing, they indulged in sinful behaviours. [74]

You can run away from the sight of people, but you can't hide yourself from the one who created the darkness. The subsequent poem is credited to Ibn al-Jawzi and expresses, "When you are alone in the dark, and the *nafs* (the self) invites you to sin, feel ashamed that Allah is watching and tell the *nafs* that the one who created the dark is watching."

73 Ibn Ḥibban, 403
74 Ibn Majah, 4245

Your true self is revealed when no one is watching except Allah. Be conscious of Him, and don't let your actions turn into dust on the Day of Judgment. When tempted to commit a sin privately, ponder on what you would say to Allah if it were to be your last action.

Fear Allah When Alone

Reflection:

Don't Underestimate Any Deed

Allah said: "... and thought it was insignificant while it was in the sight of Allah, tremendous." [75]

A prostitute was passing by a panting dog near a well and seeing that the dog was about to die of thirst, she took off her shoe, and tying it with her head-cover, she drew out some water for it. So, Allah forgave her because of that. [76]

Another woman entered the hellfire because of a cat which she had tied, neither giving it food nor setting it free to eat from the vermin of the earth. [77]

The prostitute woman who gave water to a thirsty dog did not know that her action would take her to paradise. The woman who imprisoned the cat did not know that that

75 Qur'an 24: 15
76 Ṣaḥiḥ Bukhari, 3321
77 Ṣaḥiḥ Muslim, 2619

would take her to hell. You don't know which good deeds will be your ticket to paradise and the one that may lead you to hell. Never belittle a good deed, regardless of its size, and never underestimate a bad deed, no matter how small you perceive it to be.

Don't Underestimate Any Deed

Reflection:

The Paradise On Earth

Ibn Taymiyyah (r.a.) said: "My enemies can't break me because I'm content with Allah's degree (paradise in my heart) and I see every obstacle as an opportunity." [78]

Ibn Taymiyyah is emphasising that the earthly paradise is contentment. Before attaining paradise in the hereafter, strive to achieve contentment in this world, regardless of your current circumstances and you will experience peace of mind.

Do not be burdened by the concerns of this world, as what is destined for you will reach you, and what is not meant for you will pass you by. Trust in Allah's control and wisdom, finding satisfaction and pleasure in His plans. This inner paradise will grant you tranquillity and a sense of fulfilment.

78 al-Wābil al-Ṣayyib, 1:48

The Paradise On Earth

Reflection:

GIVE CHARITY

The Messenger (s.a.w.) said: "Set up a barrier between yourself and the Hellfire, even with half of a date in charity." [79]

When the Messenger (s.a.w.) asked the Muslims to give charity, ʿUmar (r.a.) gave half of his fortune, he thought: "Today I would surpass Abu Bakr aṣ-Ṣiddiq (r.a.) in good deed". Then came Abu Bakr aṣ-Ṣiddiq to give his entire wealth in charity, ʿUmar said: "I will never be able to surpass Abu Bakr!". [80]

79 Ṣaḥiḥ Bukhari, 1407
80 Jamiʿ at-Tirmidhī, 3675

Everything you possess is a gift from Allah. Be generous without hesitation, for the more you give, the more you will receive. Contributions made for the sake of Allah are not lost; consider them as deposits into your account for the hereafter.

Give generously from what you cherish, as that is the kind of charity Allah values. Remember, the money you possess isn't truly yours; it belongs to Allah. Your wealth isn't a result of your efforts alone; others may work harder and possess greater skills yet have less. Gratitude and generosity are ways to acknowledge Allah's blessings. When you give charity, it will:

- ☑ Stand in the way of calamity.
- ☑ Be your shade on the Day of Judgement.
- ☑ Protect you from fire.
- ☑ Elevate your status
- ☑ Increase your sustenance

You can attain paradise by engaging in acts of charity and assisting those in need. Wealth isn't the sole prerequisite; your intention and eagerness to contribute hold greater significance. Don't underestimate the impact of your generosity, regardless of the scale.

Give Charity

Reflection:

SERVE OTHERS

The Messenger (s.a.w.) said: "The most beloved people to Allah are those who are most beneficial to people."[81]

True generosity is when you help someone, and you do not expect something in return; you know that the reward would come from Allah. The hands that give and help are better than the ones that receive. The Messenger (s.a.w.) said:

> "Whoever among you is able to benefit his brother, let him do so."[82]

If Allah has bestowed upon you the ability to aid others, recognise it as a valuable opportunity from Him. If you neglect to assist, Allah may provide aid through someone else. Gratitude should accompany your acts of service;

---

81 al-Mu'jam al-Kabir lil-Ṭabarani 6:139
82 Ṣaḥiḥ Muslim 2199

envision yourself in a position of need and appreciate the assistance you would receive in such a scenario.

As long as you help your brother, Allah will help you, not only in this world but also in the hereafter. The Messenger (s.a.w.) said:

> "That I walk with a brother regarding a need is more beloved to me than that I seclude myself in this mosque in Medina for a month," [83]

Allah has been good to you, don't you think it would be wise to also do good unto others? Be in service of the common good. You are a trustee of this world as was our grandfather, Adam (a.s.). Make sure to leave this world better than you found it, as a true leader serves others.

83 al-Mu'jam al-Kabīr lil-Ṭabarani 6:139

Serve Others

Reflection:

EPILOGUE

If you are reading this now, you have made it through this book, well done! Ryan Holiday, a contemporary philosopher, shared a piece of wisdom from his friend, the martial artist Daniele Bolelli: "Training is akin to sweeping the floor. Completing it once doesn't ensure a perpetually clean floor. The dust returns each day, necessitating daily sweeping."

This is the same with staying on the straight path and doing the right thing to protect your light of belief. It's not because you do good deeds today that *shayṭan* won't come back to you tomorrow, or because you passed one test, another test won't come. It's a daily struggle—every day you must keep on sweeping. Neglecting this effort may result in the rapid accumulation of dust (small sins), making it challenging to manage.

It might reach a stage where the sin becomes normalised because of familiarity, to the extent that committing it no longer evokes remorse. Always remember that Allah does not burden a soul beyond its capacity. While you may feel incapable on your own, with Allah's assistance, you can overcome. Place your trust in Allah—seek His guidance and aid.

Jaafar ibn Suleiman said: "Concern about the world is darkness in the heart, and concern about the hereafter is a light in the heart." [84] Be concerned about the light of the

84 al-Zuhd li-ibn Abi Dunya 543

hereafter, not the darkness of this world. Fill your heart with light, build your eternal life, and don't fill your heart with darkness.

We have met each other in this book, even if we may not meet in person. We all came from one soul, I love you for who you are, and I pray that may Allah help you to be successful in this world and the next.

QUIZ SECTION

MERCY

Quiz: Love Yourself:

What small step can I take to start taking more responsibility for myself?

How can I use affirmation to value and believe in myself?

How can I change my negative self-talk?

Quiz: Unlimited Mercy Of Allah:

What can I do to bring my non-Muslim friend closer to Islam?

What is the best way that I could help do it?

What is my opinion about the sinners that live in my entourage?

What can I do to help them quit their sins?

What is the best way that I could help?

Quiz: Be Merciful Towards Your Spouse:

How would I like to be treated?

How would I like my children to be treated?

How would I like my daughter to be treated by her husband?

Quiz: Be Merciful Towards Children:

What is the best way to punish my children when they misbehave?

What are the Islamic values that I can teach my children?

How can I spend valuable time with my children?

What type of person do I want my children to be?

How can I start preparing them for that?

Quiz: Be Merciful Towards Animals:

What benefits would I get from being kind to a pet animal?

Should I take a pet into my care?

How would it benefit me?

Quiz: Be Merciful And Respectful:

What is the best way to show respect the people who are older than me?

What is the best way to show mercy to the young ones?

How can I practice good manners when dealing with people?

Quiz: Be Grateful For Being A Muslim:

What can I do to preserve the guidance that Allah gave me?

Did I thank Allah for everything He did for me and my family?

What can I do to remind myself of the blessings of Allah?

Quiz: Be grateful For Your Sanity:

How can I start voluntary prayer to show my gratitude to Allah?

Am I addicted to social media or/and movies? How do I stop it?

What can I do to be mentally, physically, and spiritually healthy?

Quiz: Learn The Meaning Of The Qur'an:

What is the best way for me to start learning the meaning of the Qur'an?

How can I start learning the meaning of surah al-Fatiḥah and the other surah that I recite in prayer?

Quiz: Be Satisfied With What You Have:

Am I at peace and grateful with where I'm in my life?

Have I ever think of the people who have lesser than me?

Have I ever think about the people that are in the hospitals?

Quiz: Pain Is A Blessing:

How should I behave while being tested?

What can I do to get Allah's help during the test?

Quiz: You Are Not An Angel:

What mentality should I have after sinning?

How can I reduce my possibility of sinning?

Quiz: Change Your Life:

Do I dwell on the painful past events of my life?

How can I stop wasting time on the things that I can't control?

How can I be the best version of myself?

FORGIVENESS

Quiz: Seek Allah's Forgiveness Now:

Am I ready to meet Allah in my current condition?

Did I make enough preparation for my death?

Is Allah pleased with me at this very moment?

Quiz: Forgive Yourself:

What are the sins that I did not forgive myself for?

What can I do, to never repeat that same mistake?

Quiz: Seek Forgiveness From Those You Have Hurt:

Who are the people that I have hurt, and never asked them for forgiveness?

What is the best way for me to ask them to forgive me?

What can I do, that would never hurt them again?

Quiz: Forgive Others:

Am I holding ill feelings towards someone who has hurts me?

What benefit do I get from being angry towards something that already has happened?

What can I do so that Allah will forgive me?

Quiz: Don't Waste Your Reward:

Do I check my intention before I do any good action?

Do I genuinely smile towards the ones I'm helping?

Am I grateful to Allah for giving the opportunities to help people?

Quiz: Don't Harm Others:

Did I harm anyone in the past that I did not ask to forgive me?

Am I oppressing someone with my actions or words without knowing

Is Allah pleased with me with the way I deal with people?

Quiz: You Can't Fight Fire With Fire:

What can I do to calm down when angry?

How can I improve my communication skills to communicate better?

Quiz: Advise People Or Correct Them:

How can I help the people in my family to become better?

Do I bring people together or do I separate them?

How can I be part of the solution instead of part of the problem?

Quiz: It's Not Healthy:

Am I getting any health benefit by not forgiving others?

What can I do now to improve my health state?

Quiz: It Gives Relief:

Which one is more important? Me forgiving and living at peace or me not forgiving and having sleepless nights?

Quiz: Accept Society's Nature:

How can I start accepting people as who they are and not who I want them to be?

What can I do the next time someone hurts me?

What is the best thing for me to do in order to bring people together and not against each other?

Quiz: Don't Be Offended By The Truth:

Do I want a solution to the problem, or do I want to win the argument and be right? And why?

How can I analyse what is being said if it's true or not true?

Quiz: Don't Be Bitter:

Why do I have resentment towards people?

How can I stop holding grudges towards people?

How should I speak about what is bothering me to the other person?

Quiz: Don't Hate:

How can I stop hating those that I hate and why must I do so?

How can I control my emotions, and not let them control me?

What advice would I give my friend about hating someone?

Quiz: Don't Blame Allah:

What is the best way for me to accept what has happened to me?

How can I start seeing challenges as an opportunity for me to be stronger?

What is the best way for me to advise someone who is going through a test?

SAFETY FROM HELL FIRE

Quiz: Be Productive:

How can I be the hero of my story and not the victim?

How can I stop procrastinating and take responsibility for my life now?

Quiz: Don't Go Back To Haram:

What haram actions did I stop during Ramadan and start doing after Ramadan?

How can I stop doing it now?

How can I be among the few and not the masses?

What is the best way for me to advise my friend not to go back to haram actions after Ramadan?

Quiz: Keep On Doing Good:

What are the good deeds that I stopped doing?

Why did I stop doing them?

How can I keep them up?

Quiz: Types Of Death:

What would I do if I had only one day to live?

How can I prepare myself for death?

Am I living on what I want to be resurrected upon on Judgment Day?

What is stopping me from living according to Allah's rules?

Quiz: Be Alive:

How can I include daily remembrance of Allah in my schedule?

What can I do to encourage my entourage to remember Allah often?

What advice can I give to someone who does not have peace of mind?

Quiz: Guidance:

What can I start doing so that Allah will keep me on a straight path?

How do I protect myself from a self-righteous mindset?

Quiz: Use Your Tongue Wisely:

How can I use my words to empower people and not use it to hurt them?

How can I make it a daily habit to give charity with my tongue?

Quiz: Backbiting:

Do I backbite?

How do I stop doing it?

What's the best way to advise someone not to backbite?

What do I do when people backbite about someone in my presence?

Quiz: Protect Yourself And Your Family:

How do I protect myself and my family from the *fitnah* of this century?

Is the seed of *fitnah* already growing in my house?

How do I stop it from getting bigger?

What is the best way for me to organise a continuous hadith-reading section with my family?

Quiz: Paradise Is Under Her Feet:

How can I show gratitude to my parents for all the sacrifices that they have done for me?

What words and actions can I do to show my love to my parents?

What is the best way for me to take care of them as how they took care of me when I was a child?

Quiz: Choose The One That Will Take You To *Jannah*:

What would the prophet advise me to do if I wanted to get married?

What would I do if I were to make a choice between Allah's order and the wishes of my loved ones? And why?

Am I blinded by love that I don't want to see the truth as it is?

How can I fix it?

Quiz: Fear Allah When Alone:

What can I do the next time I feel tempted to do something haram?

What policies can I set for myself to follow in order to avoid haram?

What should I do when I find myself in the middle of a sin?

Quiz: Don't Underestimate Any Deeds:

How can I start seeing events as an opportunity to get closer to Allah?

How can I be an asset to this religion and not a liability?

Quiz: The Paradise On Earth:

Am I contented with where Allah puts me?

What is the best way to show my gratitude to Allah for everything that He gave me?

How can I control my greed so that it does not control me?

Quiz: Give Charity:

How can I start giving a monthly charity?

Who in my family/entourage is in financial need and how can I help them?

What objects I don't need or use that I could give to someone who does?

Quiz: Serve Others:

What are the gifts that Allah gave me?

How can I use my gifts to make the world a better place?

How would I like to be raised on Judgment Day?

GLOSSARY

Fajr :	Dawn prayer
Fitnah :	Tribulation
Haram :	Prohibited
Jannah :	Paradise
Nafs :	The soul
s.a.w. :	(Sallallāhu ʿalayhi wa salam) Peace be upon him
r.a. :	(Raḍi Allāhu ʿanhu) may Allah be please with him
Ruqyah:	Treating illnesses through Qur'anic ayat and invocations
Shaykh :	A leader in a Muslim community or organisation
Shayṭan:	Devil

References

Al-Albani. *Silsila Ṣaḥiḥa 1055.* Riyadh: Maktaba Maharif Linashr Watawdhih, 2008.

Al-Darimi, 'Abd Allah bin 'Abd al-Rahman. *Sunan al-Darimi.* Riyadh: Dar al-Maghni, 2000.

Al-Nawawi, Yahya bin Sharaf. *Riyad as-Salihin.* Beirut: Dar Ibn Kathir, 2007.

Al-Qazwini, Muhammad bin Yazeed bin Majah. Riyadh: *Sunan bin Majah.* Maktaba Dar us-Salam, 2007.

Al-Samarqandi, a. l. *Tanbih al-Ghafi lin bi-Ahadith Sayyid al-Anbiya' wa al-Mursalin.* Beirut: Dar Ibn Kathir, 2000.

Arifi, D. M. *Enjoy Your Life.* Riyadh: Darulssalam, 2008.

Arnold, Johann Christoph. *Why Forgive.* Farmington: Plough Publishing House, 2007.

Asakir, Ibn. *Tārīkh Dimashq 5/408.* Beirut: Dar fikr, 1995.

Baz, Ibn. *The Collection of Fatawa by Ibn Baz.* Islam Port, [http://www.islamport.com/b/2/alfeqh/fa-tawa/%C7%E1%D-D%CA%C7%E6%EC/%E3%C-C%E3%E6%-DA%20%DD%CA%C7%E6%EC%20%E6%20%E3%DE%C7%E1%C7%CA%2%C7%C8%E4%20%C8%C7%D2/%E3%CC%E3%E6%DA%20%DD%-CA%C7%E6%EC%20%.)].

Bin Hanbal, Ahmad. *Musnad Ahmad.* Riyadh: Maktaba Dar-us-Salam, 2012.

Bin Ismail, Muhamad. *Al-Adab al-Mufrad Ch 6: On Repaying Parents h11*. Petaling Jaya: Dakwah Corner Publications Sdn Bhd, 2014.

Bin Ismail, Muhamad. *Sahih Al-Bukhari.* Riyadh: Maktaba Dar-us-Salam, 1997.

Bin Qudamah, Ibn. "The Book of Repentance by Ibn Qudamah pg:124." Shamela.ws,[https://shamela.ws/book/11317].

Cassius, Dio. *Dio's Roman History*. London: Heinemann,1927.

Dehghan, Saeed Kamali. "Iranian Mother Who Spared Her Son's Killer: 'Vengeance Has Left My Heart.'" The Guardian, April 25, 2014. https://www.theguardian.com/world/2014/apr/25/interview-samereh-alinejad-iranian-mother-spared-sons-killer.

Goldman, Peter. *The Death and Life of Malcolm X.* Illinois: University of Illinois,1979.

Hanselman, Ryan Holiday. *The Daily Stoic pg:161.* New York: Penguin, 2016.

HUSEIN, Mohammed Sani. "A Study of the Approach of Shaykh Abdulhamīd Kishk in His Fī Riḥābi-t-Tafsīr." Uilspace.unilorin.edu.ng, [https://uilspace.unilorin.edu.ng/bitstream/handle/20.500.12484/7681/HUSEIN%2c%20 Mohammed%20Sani.pdf ?sequence=1&isAllowed=y].

Ibn, Asakir. *Tārīkh Dimashq 5/408.* Beirut: Dar fikr, 1995.

Ibn, Kathir. *Tafsir Ibn Kathir.* Riyadh: Maktaba Dar-us-Salam, 2003.

Ibn, Taymiyyah. "Ibn Taymiyyah on Sakinah: What can my enemies do to me?" Abuaminaelias.com, [https://www.abuaminaelias.com/dailyhadithonline/2017/06/12/hereafter-concern-nur-qalb/].

Ibn, Taymiyyah. "Ja'far on Akhirah: Worry about the Hereafter is light in the heart." Abuaminaelias.com, [https://www.abuaminaelias.com/dailyhadithonline/2014/02/27/ibn-taymiyyah-enemies/].

Ibn, Taymiyyah. *Djamih Massail 277/6.* , Beirut: Dar Ibn Hazm, n.d.

Jaku, Eddie. "TEDxTalks. The Happiest Man on Earth: 99-year-old Holocaust Survivor Shares His Story | Eddie Jaku | TEDxSydney." Youtube.com, [https://www.youtube.com/

Jordan B, Peterson. *12 Rules for Life.* UK: Penguin, 2018.

Karen, Swartz. "The Healing Power of Forgiveness." Hopkinsmedicine.org, [https://www.hopkinsmedicine.org/news/publications/johns_hopkins_health/summer_2014/the_healing_power_of_forgiveness].

Muhammad ibn, Jarir al-Tabari. "Tafsir Tabari edition:1st Vol:22 Sourat Al-Hashr: 16, pg:541." Archive.org, [https://archive.org/details/tafseer-al-tabari/taftabry22/page/n1/

Muslim bin al-Hajjaj, Abul Hussain. *Sahih Muslim*. Riyadh: Maktaba Dar-us-Salam, 2007.

Naik, D. Z. "ZAKIR NAIK: MY LIFE AND MY STORY." Youtube.com, 15 January 2022. [https://www.youtube.com/watch?v=7xDDPfTggss].

Nielsen, Katie. "8 Incredible Stories of Forgiveness That Will Touch Your Heart." Familytoday.com, [https://www.familytoday.com/family/8-incredible-stories-of-forgiveness-that-will-touch-your-heart/]. the_healing_power_of_forgiveness].

watch?v=scCvi3vY4jQ&t=627s].

Qarni, Aaidh Al-. *Don't Be Sad.* Riyadh: International Islamic Publishing House, 2005.

Sharma, Abhi. *The Great Book of Best Quotes of All Time.* Creative Commons Attribution.

Sulayman, Abu Al-Qasim bin Ahmad bin Al-Tabarani. "Al-Mu'jam al-Awsat 4/6026." Archive.org, https://archive.org/details/AlMujamAlAwsatJild4/page/n545/mode/2up.

Sulayman, Abu Al-Qasim bin Ahmad bin Al-Tabarani. *Al Mujam Al Awsat 4278.* Beirut: DKI, 2012.

Sulayman, Abu Al-Qasim bin Ahmad bin Al-Tabarani. *Al-Mu'jam al-Kabir 8745.* Beirut: DKI, 2007.

Swansea, Flamur Vehapi. *The Book Of Great Quotes.* Claritas Books, 2018.

Milton Keynes UK
Ingram Content Group UK Ltd.
UKHW021140010424
440413UK00008B/139